HAROLD WASHINGTON

"In our ethnic and racial diversity, we are all brothers and sisters in a quest for greatness. Our creativity and energy are unequalled by any city anywhere in the world." — Harold Washington

HAROLD WASHINGTON
Mayor with a Vision

By Naurice Roberts

 CHILDRENS PRESS ®

CHICAGO

Dedication: *To my mother, Mary L. Roberts,*
who is the original source of my quality, and to
the spirit and legacy of Mayor Harold Washington.

Library of Congress Cataloging-in-Publication Data

Roberts, Naurice.
  Harold Washington : Mayor with a Vision.

  (Picture-story biographies)
  Summary: Follows the life and career of Chicago's
first black mayor, assessing his impact as lawyer,
state representative, state senator, mayor, and
national leader.
  1. Washington, Harold, 1922-1987—Juvenile literature.
2. Mayors—Illinois—Chicago—Biography—Juvenile
literature. 3. Chicago (Ill.)—Politics and government
—1951   —Juvenile literature. [1.   Washington,
Harold, 1922-1987. 2. Mayors. 3. Afro-Americans—
Biography] I. Title. II. Series.
F548.52.W36R63   1988   977.3'1100496073024
[92]   [B]   88-7247
ISBN 0-516-03657-2

PHOTO CREDITS

© Antonio Dickey—1, 2, 3, 4, 5, 14, 15
   (right), 18, 20 (left), 21, 22, 23, 24, 25, 26,
   27, 29, 30, 31, 32
Courtesy Ramon Price—9 (2 photos), 10
Courtesy Roosevelt University—11, 12
© Beverly Swanagan—Cover, 6, 7, 15 (left),
   17, 20 (right), 28 (2 photos)

Quotations on pages 2, 5, 31 were taken from
   Harold Washington's inaugural address,
   April 29, 1983.

Childrens Press would like to thank the
   family of Harold Washington for its
   assistance.

"I reach out my hand, and ask for your help. With the same adventurous spirit of Jean Baptiste DuSable when he founded Chicago, we are going to do some great deeds here together." —Harold Washington

Harold Washington's supporters eagerly await election results. Mayor-elect Washington (opposite page) proclaims victory on election night, April 12, 1983.

"Here's Harold!" At the sound of his name, the crowd roared. They clapped, stomped, and yelled with excitement.

"Harold! Harold! Harold!" Louder and louder the cry rose until it shook the very room where hundreds had gathered. Every man, woman, and child there had come

together for one purpose—to elect
Harold Washington as the first
black mayor of Chicago.

Harold Washington loved politics.
He learned his first lessons about
Chicago politics from his father who
was a minister and a lawyer. As a
boy he often helped his dad pass out
handbills for the Democratic party.
The lessons he learned at his
father's side were valuable. In the
future they would help Harold
become a skillful politician and a
powerful Democratic leader.

Harold Washington was born at Cook County Hospital in Chicago on April 15, 1922, to Roy L. Washington and Bertha Jones. Eventually, the family would grow to include ten children.

Growing up around 47th and King Drive was fun, especially for Harold. His big smile and quick humor made him many friends.

Whatever he did, he did wholeheartedly. It is said that ''when Harold threw a ball from third to first, the first baseman had better brace himself or be knocked down trying to catch the ball.'' It seemed that when you dealt with Harold, you had to be strong.

In school Harold showed strong character, too. He attended St. Benedict the Moor Boarding School in Milwaukee, Wisconsin. But he missed his family and friends.

Roy Washington, Harold's father

Bertha Jones, Harold's mother

Determined to return to Chicago, he ran away one day. Soon after, he was enrolled in Forestville Elementary School in Chicago.

Later, Harold went to DuSable High School where he showed great promise as a student and an athlete. Before graduating he joined the Civilian Conservation Corps (CCC), which was like today's Peace Corps. In the corps he worked with other young men to protect America's natural resources. They planted trees, built dams, and learned about agriculture and conservation. It was

as a member of the CCC that
Harold learned the importance of
cooperation and teamwork.

   When Harold returned to Chicago
in 1942, he married his high school
sweetheart, Nancy. That same year
he was drafted into the army. World
War II had already begun. He was
sent to the Pacific where he served
in an all-black engineering and
aviation battalion.

Sgt. Harold
Washington,
U.S. Army

Harold (fourth from left), as vice-president of the student council, at Roosevelt University, 1948

While serving in the army, Staff Sergeant Washington continued his education through the mail. When he returned to Chicago in 1946, he was ready for college. He enrolled at Roosevelt University as a political science major. He had come to realize that education was the key to success.

Harold was a serious student and

an avid reader. As a member of the
debating team, he developed into a
powerful public speaker. His
leadership abilities gained him the
respect of his teachers and friends.
He was elected president of his
senior class and also became the first
black president of the student
council. Everyone trusted Harold to
get the job done. And he did.

When Harold graduated from
Roosevelt University in 1949, it was

As vice-
president of
the student
council,
Harold often
addressed
student
assemblies
and
introduced
school
dignitaries.

with honors. He then enrolled at Northwestern University Law School. This was an exciting challenge for Harold, and he was determined to succeed. In 1952, Harold earned his law degree from Northwestern and proudly became a partner in his father's law office.

As a young attorney, Harold didn't seem too interested in practicing law. He was more excited about working with his father in the 3rd Ward Democratic Organization. When his father died in 1953, however, Harold's life changed.

Saddened by the death of his father and his hero, Harold decided to continue his father's law practice and his work in the Democratic party. He became a precinct captain and then went on to become assistant corporation counsel for the city.

In 1964 Harold ran for public
office. He won a Democratic seat in
the Illinois House of Representatives
and was reelected five times.
During the twelve years that he
served as a state representative
in Springfield, Illinois, he worked
to protect the rights of the poor
and disadvantaged. He worked
to give black voters a powerful
voice in Democratic politics.

Some of the bills he sponsored were for fair employment practices, low-cost housing, fair housing practices, women's rights, and rights of the elderly and the handicapped. He also helped to form the Illinois Arts Council. And because of Harold's efforts, a bill was passed that made Dr. Martin Luther King's birthday a full state holiday.

Mayor Washington (left) hosts the Chicago celebration of Martin Luther King national holiday, January, 1985. Coretta King (right) presents Harold with a book about her husband.

State Congressman Harold
Washington was well respected in
Springfield. He became known as a
spokesperson for civil and human
rights. In the 1960s he got involved
in Chicago politics, too. He began
speaking on behalf of people who
were not receiving equal treatment
in Chicago under Mayor Richard
Daley. Harold was a Democrat but
that didn't stop him from criticizing
Mayor Daley, the boss of the
Democratic party.

In 1976 a number of civic groups
strongly supported Harold when he
ran for the state senate. Shortly after
being elected state senator, he ran
for mayor of Chicago. But Harold
did not have enough campaign
funds in 1977, and he could not get
the support he needed. As a result,
he lost.

Congressman Harold Washington poses with outgoing Congresswoman Shirley Chisholm (center) and his fiancee, Mary E. Smith in Washington, D.C., 1982.

Harold was not discouraged by defeat. He immediately set a new goal for himself. In 1980 he was elected U.S. congressman for the 1st District of Illinois. Now he would be taking the problems of the poor to Washington, D.C.

Harold was a good congressman. He was elected to a second term in

The 1983 televised mayoral debate between Harold Washington, Mayor Jane Byrne, and State's Attorney Richard Daley

1982. But when many people asked him to leave Washington, D.C. and run for mayor of Chicago, he accepted. He was convinced by his supporters that it was time for a change in Chicago politics. People who had little influence in government in the past now wanted the opportunity to share in the process of running the city.

Getting elected mayor was no simple task. Harold Washington knew he would have to run against candidates who had powerful friends in government. He also knew that many voters did not want a black man running the city of Chicago. But Harold Washington could not disappoint the people who counted on him to win. He could not ignore the dreams of those who believed that, when he became mayor, he would open the doors of City Hall to those who had been neglected and shut out.

The 1983 mayoral race was unpleasant for everyone involved. It divided the city. Some people responded to Harold's campaign with anger and fear. Others resorted to name-calling and secret deals to control votes.

Throughout the long and difficult campaign, Washington's supporters stood by him. When others were saying he couldn't win, the black and Hispanic communities were getting out votes for him. Soon leaders across the country were offering their support.

On April 12, 1983, Harold Washington's victory caught many people by surprise. He had beaten the odds and become the forty-second mayor of Chicago.

Harold gets support from a young campaigner (left) and the head of a woman's organization (right).

Harold Washington's inauguration at Navy Pier,
April 29, 1983

Several weeks later at his
inauguration he asked the citizens of
Chicago to forget their differences
and work together for a better city.
He told them that without
everyone's cooperation the city
would not move forward.

Harold loved being mayor, even though he did not get the cooperation he needed in the city council. Because there was so much disagreement in the council, the mayor could not accomplish many of the things he wanted for Chicago. But the changes he was able to make made the city a fairer place for everyone to live.

Mayor Washington presides over a city council session.

As Harold campaigned throughout the city, he became more aware of neighborhood problems.

While he was mayor, more women, blacks, and Hispanics were represented in the city council. Money for city services and special neighborhood projects was more equally distributed throughout the entire city.

In 1987 Harold was reelected. With the cooperation of the city council, many new programs were planned during his second term.

The mayor worked long hours attending meetings and conferences. He spoke with business and community leaders, as well as with children, about his dreams for Chicago.

The mayor's physician once said that "Harold loved the city of

Delighted by his gift, Mayor Washington thanks the Concerned Hispanics organization.

Chicago more than he loved himself." Often his friends would tell him to slow down. Harold, smiling, would remind them that he would have time to slow down later, since he would be mayor for twenty years. Sadly, that was one promise he would never keep.

Mayor Washington and Governor Thompson (right) open the RTA extension to O'Hare Airport.

On November 25, 1987, Mayor
Washington started his usual busy
day. He talked with community
leaders about building homes for the
poor. He also broke ground for a
new housing development. Then he
went to his office on the fifth floor
of City Hall. There, while talking
with his press secretary, Mayor
Washington slumped over his desk.
He never got up.

People were stunned by Mayor Washington's sudden death. Hundreds cried in disbelief. Many schools and businesses closed. Friends from around the country mourned his passing. As he lay in state in the rotunda at City Hall, nearly 100,000 people came to say good-bye.

Silent mourners wait in the rain outside City Hall. Nearby hang visible reminders of the city's grief.

At the time of his death, many
people believed that Harold had just
begun to accomplish his dreams.
Today those dreams live in the
hearts of others who hope to
achieve them.

Harold once said,

"I deeply believe that if you give the greatest reach of opportunities to the greatest number of people, and if you put the greatest variety of talents to work on the greatest mix of common problems, you're going to find the results surpassing anything you could have dreamed of."

Maybe one day his vision and dreams for the city he loved so much will indeed come true.

"I hope someday to be remembered by history as the mayor who cared about people and who was above all fair, a mayor who helped to heal our wounds, who stood the watch while the city and its people answered the greatest challenge in more than a century and who saw that city renewed."—Harold Washington

TIME LINE   **HAROLD WASHINGTON**

1922	April 15—born in Chicago, Illinois
1938	Attended DuSable High School
1942	Joined the U.S. Army, serving until 1946
1942	Married his high school sweetheart. (Years later, they were divorced.)
1949	Graduated from Roosevelt University with a degree in political science
1953	Graduated from Northwestern University Law School
1964	Elected to the Illinois State House of Representatives and served twelve years
1976	Elected to the Illinois State Senate and served four years
1977	Ran unsuccessfully for mayor of Chicago
1980	Elected to the U.S. House of Representatives
1982	Elected to a second term in the U.S. House of Representatives
1983	April 29—sworn in as the forty-second mayor of Chicago
1987	Reelected mayor of Chicago
1987	November 25—died in his office at City Hall

ABOUT THE AUTHOR

NAURICE ROBERTS has written numerous stories and poems for children. Her background includes work as a copywriter, television personality, commercial announcer, college instructor, communications consultant, and human resources trainer. She received a B.A. in Broadcast Communications from Columbia College in Chicago, where she presently resides. Her hobbies include working with young people, lecturing, and jogging. She has written books about Andrew Young, Barbara Jordan, Cesar Chavez, and Henry Cisneros.